BOA
EDITIONS LTD

CYBORG DETECTIVE

CYBORG DETECTIVE

POEMS BY
JILLIAN WEISE

AMERICAN POETS CONTINUUM SERIES, NO. 174

BOA EDITIONS, LTD. ❖ ROCHESTER, NY ❖ 2019

First Edition
19 20 21 22 7 6 5 4 3 2 1

For information about permission to reuse any material from this book, please contact The Permissions Company at www.permissionscompany.com or e-mail permdude@gmail.com.

Publications by BOA Editions, Ltd.—a not-for-profit corporation under section 501 (c) (3) of the United States Internal Revenue Code—are made possible with funds from a variety of sources, including public funds from the Literature Program of the National Endowment for the Arts; the New York State Council on the Arts, a state agency; and the County of Monroe, NY. Private funding sources include the Max and Marian Farash Charitable Foundation; the Mary S. Mulligan Charitable Trust; the Rochester Area Community Foundation; the Ames-Amzalak MemorialTrust in memory of Henry Ames, Semon Amzalak, and Dan Amzalak; the LGBT Fund of Greater Rochester; and contributions from many individuals nationwide. See Colophon on page 88 for special individual acknowledgments.

Cover Design: Sandy Knight
Cover Art: Jennifer Rampe
Interior Design and Composition: Richard Foerster
BOA Logo: Mirko

BOA Editions books are available electronically through BookShare, an online distributor offering Large-Print, Braille, Multimedia Audio Book, and Dyslexic formats, as well as through e-readers that feature text to speech capabilities.

Library of Congress Cataloging-in-Publication Data

Names: Weise, Jillian Marie, author.
Title: Cyborg detective : poems / by Jillian Weise.
Description: First edition. | Rochester, NY : BOA Editions, Ltd., [2019] |
   Series: American poets continuum series ; no. 174 | Includes
   bibliographical references.
Identifiers: LCCN 2019018696| ISBN 9781942683858 (paperback : alk. paper) |
   ISBN 9781942683865 (ebook)
Classification: LCC PS3623.E432474 A6 2019 | DDC 811/.6—dc23 LC record
available at https://lccn.loc.gov/2019018696

BOA Editions, Ltd.
250 North Goodman Street, Suite 306
Rochester, NY 14607
www.boaeditions.org
A. Poulin, Jr., Founder (1938–1996)

Contents

I

II

III

IV

V

Poem Conveyed

I can't say which ghost
not because I am being coy
and not because the ghost
is being coy. In the glut
of ghosts, it is hard to tell
who is speaking. I do recall
a conveyor (the ghosts
call conversations *conveyors*
as that is how they travel)
when someone
told me I ought to read
Alexander Pope
because he was disabled.
And I thought: Oh no
now Pope will warm my pillows
and pollute my dreams.
He does not speak, directly,
in the poems about it.
Pope, you could say,
conveys scoliosis
in heroic couplet,
sleight of hand, anything
to escape his body.
And now that he is bodyless,
he speaks through us.
You could say. Although
I myself have not caught
a Pope. Not that I know of.

On Closed Systems

I write to figure out
closed systems

since the doc says
I'm becoming one

and I can't find Colleen
online tonight.

Can't tell where I end
and I machine tonight.

Here's the carpenter
come to fix the rot.

Here's the hammer
ready-to-hand.

If the grip breaks
what's the hammer?

The leg w/ all
its accessories—

a spray bottle
a button to push

the air out—
unreadies me.

Is this very sexy?
No, it is not.

Did the hammer work?
It fixed the rot.

I'm worried I lost you.
I'm worried you are a person
who does not seal into leg
does not spray herself
with alcohol and water
does not beep erratically.
You are a person who
never dies on yourself.
And I swore I wasn't
going to teach you anything
when I started this poem.
I want this poem to be
for us for cyborgs b/c
all the other poems from
all the other centuries
are for you.

Some directions.

1. Get yourself a person (not your mom) through any means necessary. Tinder is fine. Grindr is fine. This person should be available for doc appointments.

2. You are thinking of the person from work and I'm sorry: Not that person.

3. This person could be the one you're already with as long as you still sleep with him/her/them. Must be a person with whom you have relations. Person with whom you put on and take off clothes. Put on and take off goals.

4. Choose your person wisely. Pick a submissive. Can't have both
   of you saying, "What do *you* want?" "No, what do *you* want?"

Entire days pass where
I'm searching
for the poet who's already

said this. Or who will
blow the shofar
in W. C. Williams' ear?

You can put it down
as a general rule
that when a poet

begins to devote himself
to the subject matter
of his poems

he has come to an end
of his poetic means
("The Poem as a Field

of Action"). Dear Williams,
Dear Very Dead Doctor,
Stop taunting me.

For you have been the authority
long enough.
For you have cruised

the hospitals and highways
for you have twaddled us
for you have thunk

"I don't know what
to write about" and put
Elsie on and took Elsie off.

For you have been in love
w/ your patients.
For you have your lips

on my ear, constantly,
like now, 12:15 a.m., Tuesday.
I'm driving the car.

The archives are full of you,
full of doctors.
Once a colleague said to me:

"I'm making an anthology
of all the poems written
by doctors and

we will go to the hospital
and read the poems
to the patients."

There's always someone
inventing a new hell for us.

Or how should I put it?
I'm worried the lyric
is insufficient. Meanwhile
across town, George
Pickering's son is on life
support at the Tomball
Regional Medical Center.
A massive stroke.

George is not invited
to the meeting in the doc's
office b/c George is
often drunk and difficult
(so *The Daily Mail* reports).
They order "terminal
weaning," which is
how the doctors say
"Poor baby, no more
breath for you forever."
Then George runs in
drunk with his gun.
Someone is shouting.
The nurse backs away.
"Squeeze my hand,"
George says to his son.
And get this: the son does.
He's not dead enough.
He's not even dying.

Other days I can mostly hide
myself from others.

Be a field of action.
When I was 18 and living in NYC

I had a friend named Patrick.
We hung out at his apartment

on Broadway and 103rd. One night
he took a call and I read his journal.

"She talks about it way too much."
Of course, I knew what he meant.

I stopped for years.
I had to become someone else,

Elsie, or else. But what if—in some
city right now—there's a woman

going to an appointment.

Strange men are presently
standing around me
in the doctor's office.

"Don't you like it?"
one of them says.
Hell, it hurts.

Enough. After
I give the speech
they are silent.

On the drive home
I realize, they like it.
The tech of it.

The money of it.
Now the men
are in my sleep:

Don't you like it.
Don't you like it.
Don't you laud us.
Don't you god us.

Catullus Tells Me Not to Write the Rant Against Maggie Smith's "Good Bones"

You don't like the poem. So what?
Why are you clicking on her, following her?

I know, I know. The metaphor sucks. So let's
get drunk. Score some poppers. Act like horses.

Call up Alec. Who is he to deprive me
of the local geraniums? Just because

he owns a thrift store. I got thrift and I got
stored in the libraries. I am checked out.

That poem is boring. It's the same poem
ya'll been writing in your centuries. Someone

gets sad, buys a house, has children, politics
and little birdies. Throw some ableism

in and publish it. Here's a poem for you.
Ignatius had a beard and I fucked him.

The Phantom Limbs of the Poets

David Musgrave has a phantom limb.
   It is the bees and a jetty.

Craig Dworkin has a phantom limb
   but he calls it a phantom shelf.
   Puts everything on it.

There used to be a zine called *Phantom Limb*.
   Is it still around? Anybody feeling it?

Nathaniel Mackey has a phantom limb.
   It's the blues and objective reality.

Ben Lerner has a phantom limb.
   It's the unavailability of the traditional lyric.

Lyn Hejinian has a phantom limb.
   It's Deleuze and Guittari's bodies.

Jay Rosenblatt's phantom limb
   is 28 mins b&w at the MoMA.

Johannes Göransson borrowed Aase Berg's
   phantom limb and now it's contaminated.

Can you guess what Albert Goldbarth's
   phantom limb is like?

Does anyone actually have a phantom limb?
   The rest of you: draw your blood elsewhere.

Regulatory Capture

For years I thought at least
the poet took the time
to call me back. Must be

a good, yes, good man.
Calls his constituents.
"Hi, Frank Bidart," I said.

I had to clear my throat.
"In one of your poems,
the speaker is an amputee

who has to pay for sex.
As an amputee myself,
I was wondering if you—"

He interrupted me to
berate me and the monologue
goes on and on

and I still hear it today.
The problem with his poem
is the problem with poetry.

I want your pain.
I'm taking it.

10 Postcards to Marie Howe

Dear Marie, I just read your poem "The Star Market" in *The New Yorker*. Felt like killing myself. Must mean it's a good poem—right? Yours, Jillian

Dear Marie, Yeah. I get it. Jesus is in a wheelchair. "Could I bear the look on his face when he *wheels* around?" Is this supposed to make me feel better? I don't want to be Jesus. Or a saint. Or stuck in your poem anymore. Yours, Jillian

Dear Marie, No. Just no. Yours, Jillian

Dear Marie, Sorry. This isn't productive. Yours, Jillian

Dear Marie, What I need is a surrogate to approach you, someone who is your generation, someone who represents the Disability Rights Movement, someone whose name you would recognize, so that person could say, "Let's have coffee." Yours, Jillian

Dear Marie, "The feeble, the lame, I could hardly look at them." Yours, Jillian

Dear Marie, Sir Philip Sidney (1554–1586) prescribes two emotive responses for the disabled subject in literature: laughing or crying. Your poem has given us the latter. Yours, Jillian

Dear Marie, What's up with the metaphors "sour milk, bad meat" to describe the disabled? Are you kidding? Yours, Jillian

Dear Marie, I too would like to skip to the future where these postcards are irrelevant b/c we are all on the same page. No one likes the poetry police. I'm not the poetry police. Did you ever think your reader might be the man coughing into his sleeve? Yours, Jillian

Dear Marie, I would like to believe you didn't really mean it. Yours, Jillian

Of the Impending Mission

It is best not to talk about this
which is why I am scribbling it
on the sole of my Manolo.
I met one of them in Plaidtown.
His hair was bleached and he wanted
to fuck Soxy but she wasn't into it,
no matter how cool he was
and I can tell you: he was pretty
cool according to himself.
One editor said, "Write a book
and don't cuss in it and don't
have any sex and if you must
have sex, then have it with
one person and let it be tragic,
for example, he is only sleeping
with you b/c you are disabled.
You are very sad afterwards
and take some time to be alone.
This I could sell." How to deal?
Thank you for your kind words
on the execution tourists.
I am nowhere near the target.

Conveyor to Jael

Two a.m. here. The neighbors sleep.
How are you? How's Heber? Any wars?
I'm reading the *Princeton Encyclopedia
of Poetry.* Looking for *disability poetics.*
I know we're here somewhere.
I talk to several of us on the phone.
I find *deep image* and *dolce stil nuovo*
and *ecopoetics.* Don't worry. I'll find us.
The books anesthetized me long ago.
Broke my heart to read Leviticus:
"No one who has any defect may come."
Oh, the poems they write about us.
Way worse than Song of Deborah.
At least she called you "most blessed
of tent-dwelling women." So why
am I bothering you about it? I looked
for a disabled woman in the Torah.
None have names. Try addressing
someone without a name.

What You Need to Know

You need to know the word perineum
so that you do not accidentally use it
when you mean proscenium.

You need to know the location
of your keys in case of an emergency.
You need to know Hebrew

and then teach me. You need
to know that I have been reading
your mind and I don't know who

Colleen is, but maybe tell her
that she really hurt your feelings.
Whatever you do, whatever

she does, whatever comes of us,
just remember to keep eating.

Evangelize Your Love

At home, a sixteen-year-old son
and window treatments and walls
to paint and "How was your day?"
On the web there are no days
and no seasons and no oil changes
for the Subaru. "No one important."
At the motel, flat pillows, a lamp
tall as his son in the corner and
a print of a sailboat. "In year three
the sex fizzled and we broke up.
Then we got married." Have you gotten
yourself into something? "Tonight
I am making your favorite dish."
News comes on, news goes off, taxes.
"At some point, he stopped kissing me
on the neck." She needs to write
her goals statement. "He promised."
More or less. "How can I live like this?"
The three of them in unison.

Variation on a Wedding

What have you done?
Gone off and got hitched
and the news

is just now reaching me
in Marfa
where I am codeined

with photos
of your wedding party.
All those lilies.

Why do this to me?
I went in search
of a symphony

and got dispatched
back to college
back to the rehearsal hall

the night I forfeited
your hard-on
so you could play scales

so you could practice
for the audition.
And did you get it?

That part you wanted.
Did you get it?

The Early American Hour

The Puritans often
thought about wolves
and thickets full of girls

figuring out how
as early as 1645.
You could pretend

not to do anything.
You could share
my firewood.

Should You Send That Text

Don't ask me. I'm terrible at it.
Last week I posed the same
question to a friend, who said

"There is nothing in it for you."
But I am in it. "Okay," she said.
"Set an alarm for two weeks

and then see how you feel."
Great advice, I said. I waited
two hours. All my alarms

were going off. So I sent it
and felt victorious and hid
under the bed next to

a dog toy, some dust and
what do you think? Is it love?

Variation on the Disabled Poet
Emily Dickinson's #745

I'm not sure what happened
in the room with the view
except I took to you

in a new way. Please wait.
I'm not finished. Let me be—
what's your word—foolish.

Now bring in the nay.
You never intended.
Never meant it. Besides

we have good god
good lives without each other.

Beside You on Main Street

We were stepping out of a reading
in October, the first cold night,
and we were following this couple,
were they at the reading? and because
we were lost, I called out to them,
"Are you going to the after-party?"
The woman laughed and said no
and the man kept walking, and she
was holding his hand like I hold yours,
though not exactly, she did not
need him for balance. Then what
got into me? I said, "How long
have you been married?" and she said
"Almost 30 years" and because
we were walking in public, no secret,
tell everyone now it's official,
I said, "How's marriage?" The man
kept walking. The woman said,
"It gets better but then it gets different."
The man kept walking.

I Want Your Fax

I want to be disability for you.
Make new signs for you.
They are saying things about us

online in their underwear.
The listserv is blowing up.
Ableist verse, ableist verse

and I'm talking to you.
I'm a green circle for you
and there you go again

into my cover letters.
Pinned your last dispatch
to my Outlook so every day

starts with you. Got your text.
Got your chat. Got your tweet.
Got you all over me.

I want to be disability for you
and capital crawl for you
and accommodate you.

What Thou Lovest

I consent to the bungalow
and the side of the road.
I consent to your *no* and *now*.

To any of your clothes, any
combo, any pronoun.
If you want my hand under

the table or the sobriety
of my spring break, you can have it.
If you say no visitation

to all the Fridays in April
or if you negotiate a shadow
treaty with all the Kellys

even then I consent.
I will refrain from saying
the citational romantic phrase.

And if there's any more
consent you need
charge it to me.

No Stopping, No Getting Off

On the highway
600 miles from home

in a downpour
I said—what?

You want to get married?
We could die here

for lack of light
for fog

or because somebody
veers into our lane.

III

Cathedral by Raymond Carver

Polyester is his favorite, second to snakeskin
and he has taken to pairing them, so you judge

for yourself what kind of impression we make
at the Officers Club. We go there Fridays,

which is, consequently, the only night he's up
for making love, because he gets drunk

and I'm tipsy too, but not as drunk as he gets.
Our bedroom backs up to the road, and so I listen

to the traffic, though it's late by that time,
by the time we get around to it, so it's one car

every three minutes. I'm on the side
by the window and the alarm clock, so take this

on good faith: one car every three minutes.
I miss driving you everywhere. With Lenny,

I sit shotgun. Because heaven knows
he's got to do all the driving. He always did.

He turned sixteen first, so by default of birth
he does the driving. When I offer to drive,

he acts as if it undermines everything.
"You want to drive?" "Yeah, I want to drive."

"Why?" "You always drive." "I like to drive."
"Okay." Most conversations end with me saying,

"Okay." No wonder, with all the time I spend
in the passenger seat, I want out the window.

We see Frank in his garage. He runs marathons.
He'll never go anywhere. He'll always be

six credits short of a master's degree:
a fact Sara reminds him of, right in front of us.

The Mendozas, next house down, keep their garage
and shutters closed. They never wave.

I hardly know them. If I'm lucky, and it's not
a Friday night, we go through security, and then

we're off base, which feels like a privilege.
I miss driving you places and not just because

of what you did while I was driving you places.
Though you were very good at what you did.

I never felt like you were doing it just to get
the job done. Though your professionalism

is commendable. You're an expert.
Your hands were made for there, while Lenny's

hands were made for, I guess, F-22 Raptors.
You're very good at it. You know you are.

I can't say it on the tape. I can't say *that*
on the tape. When you say it, it sounds good

but you can't expect me to say *that* on the tape
and then go on talking about Lenny. You gotta ask

one or the other thing of me, Robert.
I'm going to stop because it's five o'clock

and frankly, I don't want to say anything else
about Lenny and me, and I don't want

to hear anything else about how *inseparable*
you are with Beulah. If you're so *inseparable*,

where is she when you make these tapes?
I'm going to say goodbye now. It's five o'clock

and I've got to put the casserole in the oven.
Otherwise, we'll just starve.

Oh, oh, oh . . .

How was that? Did you like that? I feel silly
sitting in my apron on the edge of the bed

with the tape recorder and Lenny in the next room
watching *M*A*S*H*. Pretty silly. I feel like

it's a lot of work between us when we could
meet up at some hotel like I was telling you.

I could be in Seattle easy since I have friends
living up there. Let me think. Who have you met?

You met Martha, didn't you? Martha thinks
you're using me. I don't tell her everything,

just some things, and she thinks you're using me.
"What does the blind dude want with you?" she says.

"Maybe I'm using him." "What would you do that for?"
"Maybe I like him or maybe I like being used by him

or maybe I can do whatever I damn want."
That's how it goes with liberated Martha

and her liberated mouth. I don't care if you are
using me. I've got Lenny. Besides, if I hadn't met you

I'd still be looking for my yoohoo inside my body
when it's right there on the outside the whole time.

I went to the gyn and asked about it. I said,
"Dr. Jacobsen, mine is located on the outside."

And he looked at me like I was crazy. "Well yes,"
he said. "Everyone's is." So I said, "No wonder

I don't. The button is on the outside." And he said
ninety percent of women don't. Did you know that?

Ninety-percent. "They do it anyway," he said.
They do it looking at clocks and counting cars.

They do it clear through Friday into Saturday.
I don't have to tell you about it. You know

right where it is. How do you know about it?
Did some gal take your hand when you were

a teen and point it out? Don't tell me. I don't want
to hear about any gals, and certainly not *the* gal.

Martha is still living there near the train tracks.
She got knocked up by that guy from her work

so I'm not sure why she's passing any liberated
judgment on me. She had the baby last June

and I haven't seen it yet. I'm the godmother
and I haven't seen my godson yet.

You see how easy it would be to tell Lenny
I'm going to Seattle for the week to spend time

with my godson. There's your situation to consider,
Robert, and how you'd work that out, I don't know.

You said last tape that you'd do anything
to have a visit from me. Well then, do anything.

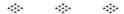

Of course I love him, we grew up together
so I thought we'd grow closer. I thought

I wouldn't be able to tell me from him
but I can definitely tell me from him

though I can't tell him. I don't know when
it happened. I don't know how you can grow

apart from someone when they're right under
your nose and grow closer to someone when

they're three thousand miles away. I don't like
living in Alabama, and I don't like being

an officer's wife, and I don't have friends here.
Yesterday we lost hot water. The hot water

went out at our place while I was in the middle
of a shower. I thought and thought of who

to call. I must've spent half an hour walking
around in my towel thinking of who to call.

There's no one. I don't have anyone to call
when the hot water goes out. I'm not trying

to be sexy here, Robert. I'm being serious.
I'm friends with Lenny's friends, sure,

I know their names when they come over
to eat dinner, play poker, watch football,

but it's not like I can call Frank and ask
to take a shower. Believe you me:

that would not look right. I'm not friends
with the wives. Lenny tells me I haven't made

enough effort. He tells me I have to put myself
out there. You know how I am.

I don't like putting myself out there.
I'd no more like to put myself out there

than step in front of a semi. You put yourself
out there more than I do. You put yourself

out there a lot for a blind guy. And why
should I make friends with the wives

when I'm not going to know them in a year?
Lenny's got an assignment in Sacramento.

The wives flocked around me when they heard
about California. "Ooo la la, Sacramento,"

they said. You'd think we were moving to Paris.
They said I'd have to get highlights and

I'd have to go tanning and I'd have to join
a gym and they got me so bent out of shape

over California I about cried. Anyway,
I'm going to leave Lenny. We need some time

apart and maybe we need eternity.
I'm coming back to Seattle. I know you don't

need a secretary now. I wish I had left Lenny
back then, like you asked, but how was I

supposed to know? If I had known the next
gal that walked into my position

would become your wife. If I had known
you were serious about me. How was I

supposed to know? I thought I had to marry
the first man and Lenny was the first man.

I know you don't believe me, but he was.
I wasn't used to anything other than

the regular yoohoo until I met you.
Why do you think it scared the bejesus out of me?

Now listen, I'm sure she's a good secretary,
and maybe a good wife, but you're full of shit,

so maybe if you love her so much you should
tell her you're full of shit. And if you don't,

then go ahead and keep on keeping on,
but I don't want to hear any objections

about me moving to Seattle. I'm calling you
when I get to town and I don't want to hear

any business on how we'll never work.
I'm not asking for work.

I understand now why you didn't want me
to come to Seattle, Robert. I get it.

Sometimes when you were talking on the tape
about illusory things, I guess I didn't pay

much attention. I didn't realize I was one
of the illusory things you were talking about,

and frankly, I had to look the word *illusory*
up in the dictionary, and I was none too pleased

to see what it means. I don't think I'm unreal.
I don't feel very unreal. I've never felt more

real before anyone in my entire life. What is it
about her? What do you like about her?

Is it how she cooks? How she smells?
If you could see her, I know that's a low blow,

but if you could see Beulah next to me,
I know you'd pick me. It's a good thing you can't see.

She's so boring to look at. She doesn't know
what to do with her hair. Even I know about hair,

like you got to wash it, comb it, dry it and do
something with it. She dresses like a grandma.

She has nothing to say. She repeats everything.
I guess a man like you doesn't need a woman

who has things to say. I guess a man like you
doesn't need a hairdo. I guess a man like you

just wants someone to stick around. Help you
cross the road. Guide the cake to your mouth.

Well, you got it. Beulah will never leave.
No one else would be blind enough to want her.

Public Ecstasy

I feel something deeply
Yeah, very deeply
The death of a beautiful woman
   is the most poetical topic
She dies tomorrow
Isn't she pretty
Isn't she athletic
Isn't she white
Isn't she dying
Is she dead yet
Everyone get online
Everyone buy something
Tell us the name of the drug
They say her name
Say her age
Say the place
Say the death date
What's the drug
So great for the Right-to-Die Movement
We can get a lot of mileage out of her
No more death
Everyone say *end-of-life*
No more birth
Everyone say *beginning-of-life*

Variants of Unknown Significance

The stalker is standing by my car.
We were near a ravine in Raleigh
and something else out of place.

All my friends are pregnant.
Standing by my car. Lost.
Looking for my office.

Direct police to the crime scene.
The baby came and then no more
going to Raleigh for parties.

The stalker is white, married
middle-age, middle-class.
That's my car. That's the guy.

And in the middle of the song
Lark's husband kissed my ear.
I don't want to do homicide.

Be in it. Then again, maybe
he's harmless. I bought
a yellow whistle, 600 mg

of melatonin and a shirt
that reads *don't hurt me.*

I Had a Little Cash

I had a little cash and I was going to buy a gun
but they said, No, you can't
They said, Believe in the police
We believe in the police
All you have to do is call them
They come running, running
I had a little cash to buy a gun
but they said, Why would you do that
Who are you to do that
We do not do that with our money
I want to raise a goat in a field
and protect the goat from a lion
If it's about animals, then may I buy a gun?
I had the cash to buy the gun
but they said, You can't you're a poet
Poets don't buy guns
So I dressed with my empty leather holster
(in truth I was thinking of some poets
just south of here who go shooting
I know I am not alone), and wore my holster
over my blue jeans and said to them
What do you want me to do
Should I wait for something to happen
Oh, you want me to run
You want me to gunless run legless across a field
Are you trying to get me killed

Attack List

Woman jammed between two doors this morning
3 men held for gang-raping a mentally disabled woman for 3 days
Sicko rapes disabled woman at the racetrack
'Faulty stair lift has left me a prisoner for almost 10 years'
Accusation doctor sexually assaulted patient
    could have been a 'ghastly misunderstanding'
Brief: Disabled woman to share her story
Disabled woman gang-raped in Cuddalore
Torture killer Melvin Knight again appeals sentence
Obstacles facing the disabled
Disabled woman so scared she hid in wardrobe
State-run residential facility sued over death of patient
'Betrayed' couple face new battle on bedroom tax
Disabled woman in all-night sex ordeal
Disabled woman's car set on fire twice
Mom pleads guilty in disabled daughter's death
Woman's mobility scooter stolen as she attends funeral
'I've been left to live in a jungle!'
Court grants new trial in sadomasochistic sex case
Former driver arrested for molesting disabled woman
NYC developer accused in disabled-access suit
Paralyzed ex-gymnast, new son doing well
Silver band official jailed for sexual assaults
Disabled woman dies in Peterborough house fire
Disabled woman rolled off platform into path of train
European court awards payout to disabled woman
Disabled woman loses appeal of court decision
Bed handles recalled due to entrapment and strangulation
4-year sentence for Springfield mall sex assault
Police look into abuse incident at Gosport
Disabled woman prostituted by family members
Intellectually disabled woman paid $1.25 an hour
    wins landmark case
Disabled woman angry at treatment by KMB

Disabled woman kidnapped and raped by Bahraini man
Disabled woman allowed to extend village home
Drug dealer assaults disabled woman in Leominster
Man is charged with beating a disabled woman
Man accused of sex slavery too ill for court
Social care fees legal victory for disabled woman
Disabled woman wins top award
Change your doctor, disabled woman told
Fugitive rapist sparks police safety warning
'We have beaten the hated bedroom tax'
Disabled woman 'trapped' in home on Christmas Eve
Man admits sex assault on disabled woman
Missing disabled woman found safe in Lake Tahoe
Disabled woman attacked from behind by robber
Staff at NY facility for disabled sued over rape
Are you disabled? Now your boss wants to know
3 plead guilty to raping disabled Alabama woman
Cyclist steals phone from disabled woman in Sibley
Man accused of assaulting disabled woman in apartment lobby
I help a disabled blond woman back to hotel
      and tabloids salivate
Thieves swap disabled woman's trike for bike
Woman shocked by random attack
Pope washes feet of disabled
Cleaner stole £3000 from disabled woman
My hellevators: wheel-chair bound woman gets stuck
Mouth, nose of disabled patient was taped
Louisiana pastor arrested for allegedly raping disabled woman
Down memory lane
Former guard denies assaulting disabled woman
'Rape victim' sues over botched police probe
Sudanese man gets 19 years in prison for raping disabled woman
'I've had enough,' says disabled woman
Woman missing from Paradise care home found dead
Disabled woman left shaken and bruised
Man assaulted disabled wife in Holton-le-Clay
Disabled lovers' plight touches the soul

Woman took her life over care concerns
Disabled woman sexually assaulted at railway station
Disabled woman to risk life in swimming challenge
Woman in wheelchair assaulted
'Horrific' beating of disabled woman
Why did courts free my ex? I said he'd rape
Disabled woman 'overwhelmed' by kindness
Great expectations
Disabled woman needs more help
Pittsburgh parking meters too tall
Disabled woman killed after 'rape'
Support worker cleared of ill-treating disabled woman
Random acts of kindness
Parents rejected disabled daughter, says surrogate
Guard guilty in second sex assault
Disabled woman is scared of city center
Carer fleeced $116,000 from disabled woman
U.S. says rapes ignored in Montana
Give intellectually disabled people a chance
Disabled woman 'wanted to strangle' rape accused
    Sunday school teacher
Fear over fees for blue badge holders
Intellectually disabled woman sexually assaulted
Another disabled woman raped and murdered in Firozabad
Man sexually assaulted disabled woman, police say
Search continues for missing woman in Paradise
Disney is sued over rules for disabled
Disabled woman 'raped' in Parsa
Pope stops his Ford Focus and gets out
    so he can bless disabled woman
Warwick woman thanks lightning Jack for help during storm
My disability helped me understand Blanche DuBois, says actor
Iowa woman overheated at group home
Disabled woman who kicked PC makes complaint
Disabled woman sues top priest
Thieves in Istanbul return stash to crippled woman
Burmese army rapes disabled woman

Patient says she tried to 'block out' sex attack
Nurse throttled brain-damaged amputee in hospital
Couple deny imprisoning disabled woman for 8 years
Pension eludes disabled woman for years
Doctors given permission not to provide life-saving care
Teacher 'hacks disabled daughter to death
    and burns her remains on BBQ'
Disabled woman escapes pipe-bomb attack in Ireland
Lowell man charged in assault on disabled woman
The death no one cares about
Man held for alleged rape of neighbor
1 dead, 2 hurt in Sumter County hammer attack
Rape charge in case of disabled Washington woman
'Boys will be boys'
Sex assaults net 5 ½ year sentence
Fitness club ordered to pay disabled woman $3,000
Disabled woman climbs Mt. Kilimanjaro
Fraudster took £31,000 from disabled woman
Teen sex beast jailed for raping disabled woman
Paralyzed 22-year-old 'raped' by peon in home for disabled
'I feel so isolated'
Pope Francis gives thumbs-up as disabled children perform
Passenger beaten up by conductor
Lord Mayor's limo forces disabled woman into road
Huge scope for recruiting the disabled

Confession

Each night the trains come.
On the night in question
the conductor laid on
the horn. I could not take it
anymore. Took the keys
from the hook, careful
not to wake Hazel.
I kept the headlights off
in my neighborhood
where a lot of people
are in my business.
I know all the 24-hour
stores and I know
she works the graveyard
and I know she parks
in the blue spot.
Her face is on the tag.
I have been disobedient.
But on the night
in question, I obeyed
the conductor who said
"Get up, get up
she's ready for you
in the parking lot."
That night I jimmied
her car door and waited
in the backseat.
I tell my wife be careful
out there. It's a jungle.

Rahab

The boys came to my house
on the edge of Prattville
and asked if I could love them
and I said I reckon I can
if you take off your shoes
and put them by the mat
and choose which one of you
goes first because no matter
what you heard I'm not like that.
They were from ten miles
or more away and had been
walking through the woods.
First I washed the first one's
feet and rubbed him
with Astrolube. Then Elroy,
who is the Sheriff, knocked
on the door and I opened
the door and he said, Bring out
them boys you got in there.
I said, Yes, I saw them
walk to the store and I saw them
talk to Aunt Evie and that's
the last I saw them.
You better hurry if you aim
to catch them. See I had
hidden them under the stairs
with the canned peaches
and coats. You better hurry,
I told Elroy. Then the boys
returned from under the stairs
and I said, Now swear
you won't kill me or my family
and they swore it.
They put on their shoes

and coats and the first one
stayed in the doorway.
Rahab, he said. Rabbit.
I'll come back for you.
I hung my lingerie
in the window
and said my prayers.
I haven't seen them since.
All my neighbors are dead.

II

Nondisabled Demands

It isn't fair to us. You owe it to the reader.
We're trying to help. We have an uncle
with a disability and he always says

exactly what it is. Take it from him.
Take it from us. Take it from them.
You can't expect people to read you

if you don't come out and say it.
Everyone knows the default mode
of a poem is ten fingers, ten toes,

in love with women and this nation.
When this is not true, it is incumbent
on you to come out and say it.

Here's what we'll do. We'll rope you
to the podium and ask
What do you have? What is it?

If you refuse to answer then we call
your doctor. Then we get to say
You're an inspiration.

Some Rights

Right to property
Right to protect property
Encrypt everything
Make private
I am so right and if I'm not
    I'm gonna burn yr FB wall down
Be something for sale
Be a strategy
Last fall was tough on us
Ask after me
Ask after me again
Small business owners
Big pharma
There are said to be 7000
    bodies buried under
    that university
If we write, it's identity
If they write, it's *Reflections*
    on American Legacy
The ADA
Those aren't just letters
Punk a bunch of coffins

Imaginary Interview

Q: Are you disabled?
A: It depends. I need context.

Q: Are you rendered incapable?
A: I am awake and sober.

Q: Are you limited by parts of the body?
A: My arms are not wings.

Q: Are you entitled to certain rights?
A: Yes, I am disabled.

Q: The U.S. Government disagrees.
A: You read the letter?

Q: *Due to the subject's advanced education, the subject is no longer disabled.*
A: It was a love letter. They could have written it better. I would've preferred something with a little more feeling, such as: "Dear Jillian, We are breaking up. We saw you outside the building with the statue of the lion. We saw you trespass through the halls and take from the shelves a number of hardbacks and take from the woman with glasses her suggestions. You have been made too erudite, too learned. If you want to protest, if you want to continue our relationship, then un-educate yourself. It would be helpful if you worked at a factory, worked at a factory, or could not find work. It would be helpful for something inside you to hurt."

Q: You seem bothered by the letter from the government.

A: They rescinded my name.

Q: The name *disability* is important to you then?

A: It is important. Very important. No, it is not important. It vexes me and I need it and I should not say it that often. Today, for example, I said: You must not use the word *disability* too much in this interview. After all, you are tired of explaining everything. After that thought came the voice of the Director, who said, "When you use the word *disability*, people think *accommodations*, people think *favors*." And after that came the voice of a writing mentor: "I just don't like the word *disabled* in this piece. Is there a way to write without ever using the word?"

Q: What is disability like?

A: It is like crowding under an umbrella, except your head sticks out, and your hair gets wet, and there are no cabs. Plus, this is somebody else's umbrella.

Q: Respond to this symbol.

A: That is where my stalker stands.

Q: What do you have?

A: I do not know. The doctors named the condition. They gave it a three-word, nine-syllable Latin name. Now I go to other doctors and they say, "What do you have?" and I say the Latin, and they say, "What?" and I repeat the Latin, and they say, "How do you spell it?" Also—and I think this is important—the prognosis for the condition reads, "No reported cases have survived past the age of two." Therefore, I am either dead with the condition. Or I am alive with a different one. Or the medical dictionary is fiction.

Q: What is the condition?
A: I am a cyborg.

Q: When did you begin calling yourself a cyborg?
A: Rephrase the question.

Q: When did you become a cyborg?
A: 2007.

Q: Where?
A: I cannot say the name of the office. The prosthetist posted a photo of me online and in the photo I am not wearing any pants. I am wearing my cyborg leg for the first time and without any pants. I am so embarrassed. I do not want you to find the photo online. This is before we knew each other.

Q: I have to tell you. When I first saw you, I thought: "She looks like a woman who could be taken advantage of online."
A: I really think, in hospitals, they should record every moment from the time anesthesia knocks you out until you are awake again. Then they should give you the footage as surveillance of their behavior, and as souvenir.

Q: Explain, if you will, how you came to wear a prosthetic, and why this leg differs from others.
A: Of course. The event. Everyone is always interested in the event. It is like a birthday party we all get to attend. The event happened when I was eleven. There was the standard preparation attendant to the event: gown, bed, alcohol, anesthesia, knife, balloons. The event occurred. As far as events go, it was a breeze. I have had several events in my life, and this one does not even rank. Everyone was pleased. I forgot: Not everyone

was pleased. The surgeon was crying. He wanted to save the leg. He had been working on the leg for eleven years. He was Pygmalion. He wanted to try his bone lengthening procedure on the leg. I said no. I said: Cut it out. Years later, the event happened again. Same leg.

Q: The same leg cannot be amputated twice.
A: Yes, I knew it would be difficult to explain. It was the same leg, the one you call *artificial* and *fake* and *prosthetic.* The one I call *my leg.* I had been wearing a series of hinge-style, basic knees. I knew the mechanics of my legs. All legs fit under the umbrella of Wittgenstein's *family of resemblances.* Then, age twenty-six, I got a new leg that required an oppositional mechanics. Electricity. It was interactive like beep, beep.

Q: How have labels of disability affected the degree to which you feel that your authentic voice has been heard by others, e.g., family, friends, health care providers?
A: "You are not." "You are, but you don't look it." "You are not enough." "I never think of you as that." "You are and you must tell us how and in what way and through a story we have heard before." "We would prefer a car accident."

Q: Respond to this symbol.

A: That is where my people park. I had to go away for a while. I wrote to them, and they wrote back: "The author does not understand the definition." I visited them, and they said, "Cyborg is a phase." I started sleeping with them and it was great.

Q: What do you want to say to the general readership?
A: Hello. May I speak to the bioethicists? Nice to meet you.

Please may I—if it is not asking too much—have permission to change the settings in my leg?

Q: We are all confused. Explain?

A: If I want my knee to flex slower on the step, I have to drive to the prosthetist's office, take off my pants, and hook up with his computer. He has the software. Since this is my leg, it is my software. How can I bring you closer to me? Let's say you purchase a BMW convertible, which costs the same as this leg. Say you want to put the top down. But in order to do that, you have to drive to the shop, talk to the mechanic, take off your pants, and then he, with his key fob, puts the top down. It is still sunny out. Are you happy?

The Responsibility of the Poet in the Voice of Ray Bradbury as Channeled by the Cyborg Jillian Weise

If you want to be a poet, Jesus God, make a list of ten things you love the most in the world. And write about them. Plug your leg into the wall and hop to it. Jesus God, you don't need legs to write poems. Have you read the poems they publish today? They're awful. Nothing happens. A dog gets shot. I love dogs as much as the next Wendell Berry. But why did the dog have to get shot? If you want to be a poet, write a poem every day. I defy you to write 365 bad poems. All this talk about the responsibility of the poet as if it's a job. Does it wear a watch? Does it require clock-in and clock-out? Does it time your lunch? Does it fire you for insubordination? I see you, the Cyborg Jillian Weise, thinking ahead to whether the readers will like this book, and wondering if—in order for them to like it, them and their friends—you need to go back and cut out all the leg parts. Jesus God, stop thinking.

Biohack Manifesto

It is terrible to be trapped at DEF CON
with not even Ray Kurzweil's
daughter to gaze upon
I know some of you wish
I would go wherever
my people go, the factory,
physical therapy, a telethon

No! says my mentor
Not this. This is too angry

This is too much about
Not that. Not that

I like to hack, sometimes,
the Hebrew Bible

I don't think my mentor hacks
the Bible b/c it has too much
lame deaf blind circumcised in it

Not that. Not that in poetry
Didn't we already have
Judd Woe? He was so good to us
so good and sad and sorry

The great thing about Judd Woe
is that now we don't have to
keep looking for a disabled poet
We got him

Everybody together now: We got him
Thank YHWH he's a man
I am so relieved, aren't you?

I am so cock-blocked, aren't you?

Here I am at the cobbler

Please, please can you make
all my high heels into wedges

Here I am at Walmart

Please, please can you make
your children stop following me

Here I am at Advanced Prosthetics

Please, please can you
change my settings

THIS IS NOT POETRY, they said

Be happy with what we give you
We got you

Insurance: You are allowed 10 socks/year

Insurance: You are not allowed to walk in oceans

Insurance: If you had fought for us, if you
had lost your leg for us, for freedom, then
we would cover the leg that walks in oceans

AND WHY IS IT ALWAYS A POEM IS A WALK?

A poem is like a walk
A poem is like going on a walk
A walk is like a poem
I was walking the other day and a poem tripped me

Don't leave
Don't I have any other ideas
Be a man, mortality, zip it

Call in the aubades
I wish I would read an aubade
Is it morning yet? This manifesto
is so so long. Too angry
Who you bangin' on my door?

JUDY GRAHN

Thank YHWH. It was getting hot in here
Ray Kurzweil's daughter is in Hawaii
I was about to give up

Yes
Yes
I know

I am trying to walk the treadmill
My leg beeps at 3 mph
This is the conference for hackers
Can somebody hack me
Can somebody change my settings

Yes
Yes
I know

JENNY HOLZER

So glad you could make it
Come in, Judy is here
What do ya'll do with all the men in our heads

Yes

Yes
It is terrible

My people are just trying to get born
like please don't test us
we are going to fail
and the test comes back
and says YOUR BABY IS FUCKED

JUDY, JENNY, I have been your student faithfully

I have kissed some ass, tho, hoping
if they like me enough—what
if they like me enough—why

JUDY, do you need a coaster?
Thy cup runneth over

The glass slipper, amenities
The manifesto must go on

BIOHACK IT

CUT ALL OF IT, my mentor says
This is not poetry

My mentor says: A poem is a walk
Get well soon, I pray for you
Must go   Poem about coed
virility   aging   dahlias

Recurrent word to describe beauty
hacked from the Hebrew Bible: Ruddy

Don't leave   In the morning
I will vacuum this up   Scansion, feet

I am sorry if you offended me
Role of disabled artist:
Always be sorry

Future Biometrics

The body that used to
contain your daughter

we found it
behind the fence

It was in a red coat
It was collected

Is she saved
Is she in the system

You're lucky
we have other bodies

to put your daughter in
Come on down

to the station

Anticipatory Action

If cyborg enunciations are the future
avant-garde, then what are real cyborgs?
Do we have to be avant or can we

be ourselves? Sometimes you all
come in and need us to assert
our powerlessness.

Of course, we trust you.
We won't ask for inclusion.
Do with us as you wish.

Or the nurse comes in and says,
"Oh no. You should have had
that shot hours ago," as if

we are responsible for time.
Call the shots. Cheap shot,
big shot, give it a shot, parting shot.

Do we count yet? Not by a long—

Notes

"On Closed Systems": George Pickering's son woke up from a "brain-dead" state after his father blocked doctors from pulling the plug on life support. This was reported in *The Washington Post, New York Daily News,* and *Daily Mail* in December 2015.

"10 Postcards to Marie Howe" clones a technique used by Joseph Grigely, a Deaf artist and scholar. Grigely wrote "Postcards to Sophie Calle" after one of Calle's exhibits. The exhibit featured photographs of Blind people. Calle had asked them, "What is beauty?" In an attempt to be inclusive, she hung their responses in Braille beside their photographs. However, the Braille was upside down.

"The Early American Hour": Thanks to Jonathan Beecher Field's talk on "Networks of Nothing: Exceptional Abstractions on the Frontiers of Early America," during which I wrote the poem. And thanks to Jonathan for early and often being an ally.

"Cathedral by Raymond Carver": The story is often taught and discussed as if the wife's relationship with Robert, the Blind man, was entirely platonic. To subvert that reading, in which the disabled person is de-sexed, the poem invents and provides the exchange on audiotapes from the wife to Robert. The language of "the wife" belongs to the story, as she is not named in it.

"Public Ecstasy": "The death of a beautiful woman is unquestionably the most poetical topic," writes Edgar Allan Poe in "Philosophy of Composition."

"Attack List": In 2013, Josef Kaplan published *Kill List* and Steven Trull published "Fuck List." These nondisabled, masculine ars poeticas contrast to the actual murders and rapes of disabled women, as reported, primarily, by media outside the United States. The beginning of the poem is published here. The poem continues online: https://twitter.com/AttackList.

"Anticipatory Action": The poem responds to Cathy Park Hong's "Delusions of Whiteness in the Avant-Garde," where she suggests "cyborg enunciations" as the future, as if we cyborgs are not already here.

Acknowledgments

Academy of American Poets: "Beside You on Main Street," "Evangelize Your Love," and "Some Rights";

The Awl: "Attack List" was published as "Attack List 2014";

Bellingham Review: "Of the Impending Mission";

Boston Review: "The Early American Hour" and "I Want Your Fax";

Drunken Boat: "10 Postcards to Marie Howe" appeared in "Cloning Disabled Subjects";

Granta: "Poem Conveyed," "No Stopping, No Getting Off," "What You Need to Know";

jubilat: "Confession";

Kenyon Review: "On Closed Systems";

The Literary Review: "Cathedral by Raymond Carver";

Narrative Inquiry in Bioethics: "Imaginary Interview";

New Republic: "Regulatory Capture";

Poetry: "Biohack Manifesto" and "Future Biometrics";

Porter House Review: "Should You Send That Text";

Salt Hill: "Rahab";

Terminus: "I Had a Little Cash";

Tikkun: "Conveyor to Jael" was published as "Dear Jael, Wife of Heber the Kenite";

Twitter: "Attack List";

Wordgathering: "Catullus Tells Me Not to Write the Rant . . ."

Thanks to Peter Conners who has given me the incredible privilege of his confidence in my work and to the BOA team for bringing it to the world. Thanks to the Lannan Foundation for a writing residency and *The Iowa Review* for an editorial residency. Thanks to the Poetry Foundation for turning "Future Biometrics" into the first 3D printed broadside with Tom Burtonwood designing it and Sean Tikkun transcribing it into Braille. Thanks to my colleagues and students at Clemson. And thanks to my family.

Many times, during the writing of this book, I've thought, "Who can I reach out to?" and Karolyn Gehrig answered the phone, and Cade

Leebron answered the phone, and John Lee Clark replied on email, and Jim Ferris introduced me to an entire disabled library in Toledo, and Sommer Browning sent a rope ladder from Colorado, and Patricia Lockwood provided the laugh in the aftermath of a dubious religious ritual, and Karrie Higgins texted back, and Jessie Male answered the phone, and Sarah Cooper answered the phone, and Aga Skrodzka said, "Why are you calling? Just come over," and Constance Merritt read some pages and showed me the shape of this book, and so did Natalie Shapero, and Meg Day introduced me to Laura Hershey, who introduced me to disability pride all over again, and goodbye Carrie Ann Lucas, we all want to call you, and Ray McManus read drafts of the poems, and Khadijah Queen went boldly with me into the *NYT*, and Margaret Price showed me how to give an access statement, and Josh Bell kept all my name-dimes safe in the storms, and Elizabeth Vogel answered the phone, and Ginna Raymer has been answering the phone since 2000. Love to Bunny. And love to Favorite Boy.

About the Author

Jillian Weise is a poet, performance artist, and disability rights activist. Her previous poetry collection, *The Book of Goodbyes*, won the 2013 Isabella Gardner Poetry Award from BOA Editions and the 2013 James Laughlin Award from the Academy of American Poets. Her speculative novel, *The Colony,* features the characters of Charles Darwin, Peter Singer, and James Watson. Her first book, *The Amputee's Guide to Sex*, was reissued with a new preface in 2017. She has written about being a cyborg for *Granta* and *The New York Times.* She created the web series "Tips for Writers by Tipsy Tullivan," which has been cited by *Inside Higher Ed, Electric Literature,* and *BOMB.* She performs the heteronym across social media.

BOA Editions, Ltd., American Poets Continuum Series

Colophon

BOA Editions, Ltd., a not-for-profit publisher of poetry and other literary works, fosters readership and appreciation of contemporary literature. By identifying, cultivating, and publishing both new and established poets and selecting authors of unique literary talent, BOA brings high-quality literature to the public. Support for this effort comes from the sale of its publications, grant funding, and private donations.

*The publication of this book is made possible, in part,
by the support of the following individuals:*

Anonymous
Angela Bonazinga & Catherine Lewis
Gary & Gwen Conners
Alison Granucci
James Long Hale
Sandi Henschel
Grant Holcomb
Jack & Gail Langerak
Joe McElveney
Boo Poulin
Deborah Ronnen
Steven O. Russell & Phyllis Rifkin-Russell
William Waddell & Linda Rubel
Michael Waters & Mihaela Moscaliuc